COOKING BY THE CARDS

RENA WINTERS

CONTENTS

Chicken Dinner

Preheat the oven to 275°F.

Use a cut-up chicken, wash and pat dry. If your chicken is from a modern grocery store, it is probably over a day old, so you must soak the pieces in cold water with one tablespoon of salt for two hours. Pat dry.

Dredge the chicken with 1/2 cup flour and 3 tsp salt, then dip in buttermilk and again in flour.

Put 3 tbsp of Crisco, olive oil, or peanut oil if you prefer the taste.

Put the oil in the pan.

Lightly brown all pieces over low to medium heat.

Remove pieces and set them aside.

Discard the grease and wipe the pan, leaving any light brown crumbs behind. If the crumbs are burned or even dark brown, discard them.

Return chicken to the cleaned pan.

Cover tightly with lid.

Bake for 45–60 minutes

The process should take about one hour, plus or minus.

There should be no pink showing, and none burned or hard. If you cover and cook slowly at a lower temperature, the chicken will be tender.

ACE OF DIAMONDS

(REGARDING A LETTER)

Rock Cornish Hen

Heat oven to 550°F, then turn the heat down to 300°F.

Place aluminum foil in pan and spray with non-stick cooking spray.

Place hen breast up. Sprinkle with favorite seasoned salt and place some inside the cavity.

I use regular salt here.

Bake for 20 minutes.

Turn the hen over and bake 10 minutes uncovered.

Turn hen over again, close the aluminum foil tightly, and bake an additional 35 minutes at a lower temperature of 275°F to 300°F.

For added taste, add 2 tbsp of your favorite jelly,

Add one half cup of fruit juice – peach or apricot

1/4 tsp Kitchen Bouquet (optional), and 2–3 tbsp water to the juices.

Correct seasonings to taste. Stir and serve over the hen.

ACE OF CLUBS

(HAPPINESS AND PROSPERITY)

Meats Using Wine And Whiskey

(INSTEAD OF SALT)

To cook a meat roast, first, lightly brown all sides of the roast.

Browning sears in the juices. Remove from pan and save juices.

Return meat to pan.

In a bowl, combine:

- 1/3 cup whiskey or your choice of 1 ½ cup white wine (remember other wines may leave a taste that distracts from the meat.)
- 1 ½ tsp Kitchen Bouquet or 1–2 beef bouillon cubes. These are very salty, so best to use tsp pan juices.
- If not enough juices, use Kitchen Bouquet and bouillon cubes and some water to increase.
- 2 tsp yellow mustard
- 1/2 tsp thyme

- 1/2 tsp pepper to taste
- 1 tsp paprika
- 1 tsp ground oregano
- 1 cup diced onions or a pinch of onion powder
- 1/2 clove of garlic or pinch of garlic powder
- 2 stalks of cut up celery and some leaves from the celery

Pour the liquid and vegetables over the roast. It should cover half of the roast.

Bake covered until done to your choice of tenderness.

Use of alcohol: It tenderizes the meat and adds tangy (not alcohol) flavor, and reduces the need for salt. The little bottles of wine come in 4 packs and are easy to store. Needs less room and stays fresh. A half bottle is perfect for most roasts.

Use 1/4 small bottle of wine for pork chops and or chicken. When the meat is done, taste the sauce and add seasoning. You should not be able to taste the alcohol.

Disaster Dinner

Can be cooked outdoors over an open fire if necessary, otherwise in the house in a pot.

Use a large pot.

Add enough water to boil several pounds of meat. You are boiling dinner including the water. Add meat ground or chopped.

Skim grease frequently.

Add vegetables, cut celery, cut onion, cans of tomatoes, green beans, yellow beans, carrots. You can use fresh or frozen vegetables.

Add 2–4 bouillon cubes or some Kitchen Bouquet.

Add seasonings to taste, salt, pepper, hot sauce, thyme and rosemary

Add additional water to come near the top of the pot.

Bring disaster pot back to boil and cook all contents for at least 20 minutes in a rolling boil.

NOTE: In the event of an actual disaster use only water that has been boiled so that it is free from contaminates.

KING OF CLUBS
(IMPORTANT MAN)

Potato Pie

Make a crust of peeled and boiled potatoes, mashed finely.

Add a little salt and stir.

Firmly pack the mashed potatoes into a buttered pie tin, to a little over 1/2 inch thick.

Peel and slice several apples, enough to cover top of mashed potatoes.

Pile the apples on top the potato crust. Sprinkle some sugar generously on top.

Bake at 350°F until apples are soft and crust is brown on the bottom.

Raw potatoes may be used in place of the cooked ones. Grate the peeled potatoes and place on a towel. Quickly squeeze out some of the moisture. Apples will be moist, but the potatoes should be dry.

Add 1/2 tsp of salt and 1/2 tsp of baking soda.

Stir and line the pie pan, pack the potatoes down firmly.

Then add apples and sugar as above.

KING OF SPADES
(INVESTMENT)

Scalloped Potatoes

Do not use packaged potatoes. They are full of preservatives and hidden fats and sugars.

Slice 2 or 3 large potatoes to make your servings.

Boil in water until partially cooked. This can be done in the microwave. Drain

Place potatoes in oven proof dish and add low fat milk to cover the potatoes Add spices of your choice:

- Salt and pepper
- Onion powder
- Garlic power
- 3 drops of hot sauce
- 1/4 tsp yellow mustard

Place in moderate oven, 275, and bake uncovered until potatoes are almost done, Do not over bake.

Add slices of cheddar cheese to cover the potatoes.

Cover the dish with a lid and return to oven. Continue baking until cheese is melted soft (you must cover the dish or your cheese will be brown and hard.)

Serve hot.

KING OF HEARTS
(RELIABLE PERSON)

Baked Corn Casserole

Use 9" baking dish

2 medium sized cans of creamed corn

Add to creamed corn

Two beaten eggs

½ cup cream or milk

Salt and pepper to taste

Use a buttered baking dish and pour in the mixed batter and bake in a moderate oven 275

until set – about 45 minutes.

KING OF DIAMONDS

(GOD WILL HELP)

Sweet Potato Pie

- 2–1/2 cups cooked and mashed yams.
- You can peel and boil or bake with the skins on which will give more food value.
- 1/3 cup sugar
- 1/3 cup brown sugar
- 1/2 tsp melted butter
- 2 eggs
- 2 tbsp molasses
- 1 cup cream or milk
- 1 tsp cinnamon
- 1/2 tsp ginger
- 1/2 tsp allspice
- 1–1/2 tsp commercial pumpkin pie spices
- Dash of salt
- Beat well and pour into unbaked pie shell
- Bake at 350 for 45 minutes

QUEEN OF SPADES
(REGARD MISFORTUNE AS PAST)

Beef With Spices and Cream

- 2 lbs. beef chunk or round steak cubed serves 4
- 1 cup sliced onion
- 1 clove garlic minced
- 1/2 cup cat sup
- 2 tbsp Worcestershire sauce
- 1 tbsp brown sugar
- 1/2 tsp salt
- 2 tsp. paprika
- 1–1/4 tsp. hot mustard
- 1–1/2 cup water or beef stock
- 1/2 cup cream or milk added last

Throw everything together, except cream or milk, and cook on top of stove until coated.

Cover and cook in oven low heat until meat is tender for about 1 hour. 300 degrees

Remove from oven and add 1/2 cup cream or milk to taste. Stir.

Do not boil the cream or milk. Add a tablespoon more of cream or milk if needed for sauce.

Serve over rice or your choice of noodles.

QUEEN OF HEARTS

(FAITH AND CONFIDENCE NEEDED)

Orange Chicken

- 1 cup orange juice concentrate or 1 cup of orange juice
- 2 tsp yellow mustard
- 1 bouillon cube or ½ tsp Kitchen bouquet
- 2 tsp sugar or sugar substitute
- 2 tbsp vinegar
- 1/2 cup sliced onions
- 1/2 cup sliced celery

Use skinless chicken breasts and place in pan. Combine in a bowl:

Pour enough water in the pan to cover the chicken.

Cover the pan and cook on low heat on top of the stove, turning chicken once.

Chicken is done when it is tender.

Does not take long.

It is done in about 25 minutes or when fork easily goes all the way through the meat.

Serve over rice.

Leftovers can be used for sandwiches.

Idiot Chicken

Wash a good sized, plump chicken and pat dry. Place in heavy oven proof pan and pour 8 oz. Sweet white wine over the chicken.

Sprinkle with seasoned salt, if desired.

Place a teaspoon of salt, one or two celery stalks and ½ onion in the cavity.

Place uncovered chicken in preheated oven at 250°F for 4 – 5 hours or longer which will depend on how big your chicken is.

Large chickens should cook 6 hours.

When you come home a wonderful smell will be in your house and you will love the tender juicy chicken that even "no-cook" people can do.

QUEEN OF CLUBS
(PROPERTY GAIN)

Country Potato Soup

- 8 medium sized potatoes cut in 1"- 2"
- 2 tbsp. butter
- 1 small onion cut up
- 1 tsp. salt
- 1 stalk celery cut up
- 3 cups milk
- Pepper to taste
- 1/3 tsp dill
- 1/4 tsp celery salt
- Pinch of garlic salt

Boil potatoes, onions, and celery until tender.

Drain MOST of the water but not all, and remove from heat.

Mash the potatoes and onions and celery leaving large lumps of potatoes in the same pot. adding the remainder of the spices, dill, celery salt, and garlic.

Add the milk

Return to heat and warm the soup. Do not boil or the milk will curdle.

Serve hot.

Serve with mint, or parsley. Nice with hot rye bread.

JACK OF CLUBS
(ADVANCEMENT)

Cucumber, Cottage Cheese, Lime Jello

- One 3 oz. package lime jello, dissolved in
  1 ½ cup boiling water
- 1 ¼ cup low fat cottage cheese
- ¾ cup grated cucumber, no seeds
- 1 cup fat free mayonnaise
- Juice of ½ lemon

Dissolve the Jello and let cool a little, 20 minutes.

Add the mayonnaise and stir with wire whip until dissolved.

Combine the cottage cheese and grated cucumber and add to the jello.

Add the lemon juice.

Refrigerate 2 hours, stirring several times while setting to make sure ingredients are incorporated.

Note: You can add a half teaspoon of horseradish to the jello for an extra kick.

JACK OF SPADES

(LOST – OR A LOSS)

Best Broccoli Salad – Hot or Cold

For Cold Salad:

Use half of a large package of frozen broccoli florets. When thawed, they will be softer than fresh ones but still crispy. If you use fresh broccoli, douse the florets in boiling water for 3-4 minutes. Chop large, but still bite-sized pieces

Dressing:

- 1/2 cup fat free mayonnaise
- 3 tbsp vinegar
- 1/2 cup nuts
- 1/4 cup bacon crumbs
- 3/4 tsp curry powder, if you like it hot, use 1 tsp curry powder or 1/2 cup raisins
- 1/2 cup chopped celery
- 1/3 cup sugar (scant) or artificial sugar to your taste

Double the recipe if you use the whole bag of frozen broccoli pieces.

Can be made ahead of time and refrigerated for several hours.

For Hot Vegetable:

Use a whole bag of the large broccoli florets, or use fresh broccoli cut into pieces

Boil the pieces until firm but tender, longer than 5-10 minutes

Prepare the above sauce recipe separately and heat on the stove just until bubbly.

Pour over the broccoli and toss to coat. Serve immediately.

JACK OF HEARTS
(SOMETHING FOUND)

Hot Rye Crisps

- 1/2 cup Parmesan cheese, grated or commercial.
- 2 tbsp chopped parsley
- 1 tsp chopped chives or 1/2 tsp onion salt
- 4–6 drops of Worcestershire sauce
- 1–2 drops of hot sauce
- 2 tbsp mayonnaise

Mix well.

Spread mixture on small cocktail rye breads on flat cookie sheet.

Place in oven at 400 until cheese browns and bubbles. Remove from oven.

Serve immediately.

JACK OF DIAMONDS

(SOMETHING GAINED)

Guacamole

- Mash 2-3 ripe avocados
- Add juice of ¼ to ½ lemons to prevent the avocado from turning brown.
- Add ¼ to 1/3 cup mayonnaise
- Add 1/8 tsp salt and a dash of white pepper.

Combine well and serve on lettuce.

Watermelon Pickles

Choose a watermelon with a thick WHITE rind, with no blemishes on the green part to touch the white part.

Cut off the white part, no red or pink or green part of the watermelon rind is used.

Cut the white rind into cubes. You should have maybe 3 lbs. Make a brine of 2 tbsp of salt to l qt. of water.

Cover and soak the rind overnight.

Drain Cover with fresh water and cook 10 minutes or until tender Drain. In large pot put 3 cups sugar 2 cups cider vinegar 1 cup cold water 1 slice of lemon

Dash of salt 1/2 tbsp whole allspice l or 2 cinnamon sticks. Place in sack tied with string 1/2 tbsp. whole cloves

Heat till the sugar is dissolved, then cook the watermelon rinds in the sugar syrup until transparent, about 45 minutes.

Remove the sack of spices, discard. Drain the pickles and store in a clean container with enough of the syrup to cover the pickles.

In today's world, you may freeze them.

TEN OF SPADES

(MISFORTUNE OR FRUSTRATION)

Lettuce Sauce Over Fresh Lettuce

Fry bacon—about 4 slices, set aside to drain.

Pour off all the grease except 3 tbsp

Add 1 tbsp of flour and 3 tsp. sugar

Stir to cook the flour on low flame to make a roux.

Beat together:

- 5 tbsp vinegar
- 1 egg
- 1 cup cold water

Add the liquid to the roux and bring to boil stirring constantly until just a little thick with no lumps.

Crumble the bacon and add to the sauce.

Pour over cleaned lettuce, cut in large pieces.

TEN OF CLUBS

(LARGE AMOUNT OF MONEY)

Cucumber Salad

Use only RIPE cucumbers

Peel and use only white interior. If you cannot find fresh cucumbers, forget it.

If you don't like the seeds, scrape them out.

¼ cup of heavy cream or milk, non-fat milk if on a diet, but use only ¼ cup as there is so much water in cucumbers.

2 tsp sugar (may use artificial sugar if desired)

1 tsp white vinegar

2 tsp apple cider vinegar

¼ tsp salt

Pepper if desired

Stir sugar, vinegar, apple cider and pour over cucumber

Add ¼ cup chopped celery and stir together.

TEN OF HEARTS

(GREAT HAPPINESS)

Candied Walnuts

Crunchy, not-so-sweet candy with a touch of cinnamon. Very easy to make, so make lots because they won't last long when guests arrive.

- 1 cup sugar
- 1/4 cup hot water

Boil together until it strings a thread when lifted by a spoonful or until it forms a soft ball in cold water.

Add 1/2 tsp. cinnamon and 1 tsp vanilla

This will make it bubble, so stir it in.

Quickly pour syrup over 1–1/2 or 2 cups of walnut halves. Stir together until nuts are well coated.

Work quickly as the syrup will cool fast.

Quickly place the nuts on a piece of waxed paper and immediately separate nuts with two forks. Once the candy crystallized, the nuts are stuck and you will not be able to separate them. Work fast. Cool and serve. They can be stored.

NINE OF HEARTS

(WISH COME TRUE)

Winter's Best Gingersnaps

- 2 cups sugar 2 eggs
- ½ cup molasses
- ¾ cup butter
- ¾ cup shortening 4 cup sifted flour 2 tsp
  baking soda 2 tsp cinnamon 2 tsp cloves 2
  tsp ginger

Mix butter, shortening and sugar and cream until light. Add eggs and molasses, mix well.

Sift dry ingredients and gradually add.

Beat hard. Mixture will be soft.

Refrigerate a spell before rolling.

Roll pieces size of walnuts in palms of hands, then roll in ¾ cup of sugar until coated.

Place 2 inches apart on greased baking sheet and bake until brown at 375 about 10 minutes.

NINE OF DIAMONDS

(MONEY)

Spiced Peaches

Moderately ripe peaches about 8 – 12 small to medium size.

Immerse in a large pot of boiling water just long enough for the skin to come off easily.

Take the skin off. Set aside.

You may wish to halve the fruit and take out the pit (optional)

Prepare liquid:

- 2–1/2 cup sugar
- 2 cup white vinegar
- 2 cup water
- 1/2 lemon sliced to keep fruit from turning brown.
- 6 cinnamon sticks
- 1 tbsp whole cloves and 1/2 tsp allspice
- 2 tsp whole ginger cut up (optional) (may use candied ginger) Heat until dissolved

Add fruit and cook just until fruit is soft but not coming apart Remove from heat

Discard the lemon

Take out the spices, If you leave a few it's okay.

Place fruit in a container with enough syrup to cover.

Spiced peaches can be frozen.

NINE OF CLUBS
(LOVE)

Walnut Clusters Chocolate Cookie

- 1/2 cup sugar 1/4 cup butter
- Cream well
- Add 1 egg and beat well
- Add 1–1/2 tsp vanilla and mix
- Melt 2 squares of semi-sweet chocolate and add to the creamed batter.
- Add 1/2 cup sifted flour and 1/4 tsp baking powder l/2 tsp salt

Sift together and mix

Add dry ingredients to the batter, mix well.

Fold in 2 cups walnuts. You must us the entire 2 cups as it is the nuts that will hold the cookie together.

Drop by teaspoons about 1 inch apart on a greased cookie sheet Bake 10 minutes – NO LONGER – at a moderate oven 325. Cookie will be soft, so remove with care to a wire rack and allow to cool completely.

NINE OF SPADES

(UNFORTUNATE OCCURRENCE)

Gingerbread Person Cookies

Cream 1 cup butter 1 cup sugar 1 cup of molasses 2 tbsp of vinegar and beat well

Sift together 4 cups of flour, sift an additional cup and have ready as a fifth cup is used.

1–1/2 tsp baking soda 1/2 tsp salt 2–1/2 tsp ginger (use 3–4 if you like the taste, we did) 1 tsp cinnamon 1/2 tsp allspice

Stir flour mixture into batter, then mix in the fifth cup – difficult On a very floured surface, roll small amount of dough to 1/8" Cut with favorite cutter

Place 1" apart on greased cookie sheet

Bake 325 for 5–6 minutes.

A 5 minute bake will leave a soft center.

A 6 minute bake will be crisper.

Plain Icing:

- 1 cup powdered sugar

- 2–3 tbsp milk
- 1/4 stick butter
- 1 tsp vanilla

For a big batch, make the icing pouring consistency.

Line cookies up on wire rack and pour.

Have waxed paper beneath, use again.

Fudge Icing or Fudge Candy

2/3 cup cocoa 2–1/4 cup white sugar 1/8 tsp salt 1–1/2 cup milk or very light cream. I do not recommend today's whipping cream or heavy cream. The icing will get too hard too fast before the sugar is cooked and it will crystallize.

Cook in a large, heavy, pot to the soft ball stage - when a teaspoonful can be dropped into a cup of ice water and it balls.

Stir often while cooking over medium to low heat. All the lumps of cocoa must be dissolved. The sugar has to be melted. You pretty much have to stand close to it, stirring it. Dot not burn it, chocolate mixtures burn easily. They also boil easily.

Remove from heat at the soft ball stage. This is repeated, but this goo has to be cooked and stirred and cooked and stirred, long enough to make an actual ball. The ice water can be slightly

Discolored from the cocoa, but it the ball falls apart and the water is dark, thus disintegrating the ball when swished around, it is not done. Cook it longer.

Then remove from the heat and add 1/4 cup butter 1 tsp of vanilla. This will bubble, don't despair. Beat with a large spoon until the icing loses its shine. If it just looses its shine, does not reflect anymore as you look across the top.

Put the cake on a rack with a platter beneath it. Quickly pour the icing over the cake, catch extra on the platter below. Cake will drip with goodies.

Perfect icing should be dry and somewhat firm on the outside and soft in the middle.

A better way to beat this stuff, is to use your Kitchen Aid mixer with wire whisk. It will be done in half the time. I have used a hand held mixer, but use a large bowl because it splatters. When using mixers, watch the surface closely. Very difficult to see if the icing is losing its shine and is therefore ready to ice the cake.

If the surface is still shinny, it is not icing at all and still syrup. Beat it more. If it hardens and cracks you now have fudge you have cooked and beaten it too much.

EIGHT OF CLUBS

(WISDOM NEEDED - BEWARE)

Low Fat Carrot Cake With Cream Cheese Filling

Using Cuisinart with grater blade, or grate by hand 3 to 4 large carrots, enough to make 3 cups. Remove the carrots and set aside.

Remove the grater blade and replace with the steel blade and add 4 – 6 large pitted prunes and whirl until barely chopped. Remove from bowl and place with the carrots.

If you do not have prunes, then add ¼ cup raisins. Do not chop the raisins, add them last.

Place 1/2 cup diet 7-up, or water, or unsweetened pineapple juice in Cuisinart bowl.

Add 1/4 cup oil (You can also use ½ cup applesauce)

Add 3 egg whites, one at a time and whirl

Add 1 whole egg and whirl to mix.

Add 2 cups flour sifted a little at a time to incorporate

1–1/2 tsp cinnamon

½ tsp ginger

¼ tsp allspice

2 tsp baking powder

1–1/2 tsp baking soda

1 tsp salt

¾ cup sugar

Return the grated carrots and prunes to the Cuisinart and whirl until they are small bits. Do not over beat as it will cause the cake not to rise properly. Add nuts and raisins if desired.

Pour into 9 or 10" spring form cake pan, sprayed with cooking spray.

Bake 325 or 350 for 45 minutes until done when tested. Cake will be moist. Loosen sides of pan, let cool completely in pan.

When cake is cooled, slice in half and fill. Can decorate top with a little sprinkle of powdered sugar if desired.

Filling:

- 8 oz. fat free cream cheese
- 2 tsp vanilla
- Use enough unsweetened pineapple juice or diet 7-up to moisten it.
- Add 3 /4 cup canned unsweetened crushed pineapple, drained well.

Stir and fill the bottom half of the cake.

Replace top and decorate as desired.

EIGHT OF DIAMONDS

(BUSINESS FINANCIAL – OR POSITION)

Strawberry Chiffon Pie

Mash 1 cup strawberries and add enough water to make 2/3 cup

Slice an additional 2 cups strawberries and refrigerate.

Dissolve one 3oz. package of strawberry gelatin in 2/3 cup boiling water

Add 2 tbsp lemon juice and the mashed strawberries only.

Chill until partially set.

Then beat until light and fluffy

Gradually add 1/4 cup sugar

Beat 2/3 cup whipping cream until stiff and fold in the strawberry mixture

Chill until the mixture mounds when stirred with a spoon, and then fold in the sliced strawberries, no juice.

Chill 4 or 5 hours

Serve with additional berries if desired

EIGHT OF HEARTS

(GOOD LUCK)

Pineapple Cream Cheese Cake

- Sift together 2–1/4 cups cake flour
- Add 2–1/4 tsp baking powder
- 1/4 tsp salt
- Cream 2/3 cup Crisco (no oil)
- 1 cup sugar and beat until light and fluffy
- Add 4 eggs and beat 2 full minutes
- Add flour mixture alternately with 3/4 cup milk and beat well after each addition
- Add 1/4 cup oil (not olive oil)
- Add 1 package of Dream Whip Powder (not cool whip which is solid)
- Beat an additional 1 minutes
- Add 1–1/2 tsp vanilla and mix well
- Pour batter into two pans (9" layer pans) greased and floured
- Bake at 300 for 20- 30 minutes until done when tested.
- Cool completely
- Fill with pineapple cake filling.

Pineapple Cake Filling:

- 2/3 of a large can of crushed pineapple and juice
- 1/3 cup sugar
- Dissolve 2 tbsp flour in
- 1/3 cup water and add to pineapple

Cook until thick, 6 – 7 minutes, stirring consistently

Remove from flame and add

- 1/3 stick of butter or margarine

Cool before spreading on first layer of cake Top with other layer and ice cake as follows:

Cream Cheese Icing:

- 2 large packages 8 oz. Philadelphia cream cheese softened very well
- Beat in 2 8 oz. cartons of commercial sour cream
- Add 1–1/4 cup confectioner's sugar (powdered) or sweet to your taste and spreading consistency Ice the cake and include the sides

Optional:

- Press coconut around the sides of the cake

SEVEN OF CLUBS

Bundt Cake With Spice

- 3/4 cup oil (similar to Wesson.

Do not use olive oil, or canola oil. The cake will not rise properly.

Add:

- 1 cup sugar
- 3 eggs
- l tsp. vanilla

Combine and beat for 3 minutes

Sift:

- 2 cups flour
- 6 tsp baking power
- 1/2 tsp baking soda
- 1 tsp cinnamon
- 1/4 tsp cloves
- 1/2 tsp nutmeg
- 1/4 tsp allspice

- 1/4 tsp salt

Add dry ingredients alternately with:

- 1 cup buttermilk.

(May use 1 cup regular milk with 1 Tbsp. vinegar)

Stir, and let stand few minutes.)

Or, use the commercial powdered buttermilk mix, available in a can.

Do not use yogurt. Cake will be too moist and not light.

- Add 1/2 cup chopped nuts.

Spray Bundt pan with Pam or other release agent.

Fill and bake moderate oven 350, until toothpick comes out clean out clean, about 35 or 40 minutes.

Low Fat Cheese Cake

Use a Cuisinart machine with steel blade, or use a heavy beater.

- 1- 8 oz fat free cream cheese
- 1- 8 oz. regular cream cheese
- 1 carton 8 oz. low fat cottage cheese small curd
- 1 lemon juice
- 1 carton 16 oz. fat free sour cream
- 5 tbsp flour
- 1 tsp vanilla
- 1-1/2 tsp. baking powder
- 2 whole eggs and
- 2 egg whites
- 1 cup sugar

Dump everything into the Cuisinart and whirl until all is mixed

When completely smooth, pour into a prepared pie crust and Bake 350 about 1 hour and 15 minutes.

This may be baked as a cake or you may use the graham cracker crust of your choice

If pie dough crust is used, you. must cover the edge of the crust or it will over brown.

When done, leave the oven propped open and allow pie to cool in the oven.

This prevents it deflating badly.

If baked as a cake, you can fill the dent on the top with crushed pineapple cooked with a little cornstarch and 1 tbsp sugar

Allow sauce and cake to cool, then spoon pineapple sauce over cake and serve.

SEVEN OF DIAMONDS
(WINDFALL)

Yellow Cake With Filling Options

- 3/4 cup butter
- 1-1/4 cup sugar
- 1-1/2 tsp vanilla
- 1/8 tsp almond extract (scant, as this is very strong)
- 1/8 tsp lemon extract (we are talking about drops here)
- 3 eggs
- 2-1/4 cup sifted flour
- 3 tsp baking powder
- 1/8 tsp salt
- 1 cup milk

Beat sugar and butter for 2 – 3 minutes.

Add the flavorings

Add the eggs and beat an additional 3 minutes more

Sift the dry ingredients and add alternately with the milk.

Pour into prepared pan and bake 275° for 1 hour and 10 minutes, or until toothpick comes out clean.

Let cool.

Cut in half and fill.

Cake Filling:

- 3/4 cup water
- 1/2 cup raisins (may use golden raisins if desired – gives a pretty glow)
- 1/2 cup chopped dates
- 1/4 cup sugar (scant, especially if the dates are commercial product with sugar coating)
- 2-3 tbsp finely chopped candied ginger 1 tbsp. flour

Cook until bubbly – about 10 minutes.

Stir in 1 – 2 tsp lemon juice

Add a tiny pinch of nutmeg

Set aside to cool. Do not refrigerate, it gets too stiff. Spread on bottom half of cake.

Return top half and sprinkle with powdered sugar (optional).

SEVEN OF SPADES
(HAPPY TIME)

Two Crust Pie Dough

Sift together twice:

- 2 cups of flour
- 1/2 tsp salt
- 1-1/2 tsp. sugar
- 1 cup shortening

I use Crisco in the can, as I have found it to be consistent over the years.

I do not recommend use of the Cuisinart as it is too easy to over mix this dough.

1/4 cup cold water (put an ice cube in it to make sure it is cold)

Put flour mixture in a bowl and cut in the shortening with knives or a pie crust cutter until it resembles coarse meal.

Sprinkle the cold water over the dough and mix with fork or pie crust cutter.

(Dump all the water in at once.)

Most recipes say to sprinkle the water over a spoonful at a time while mixing with a fork.

I find it too tedious and too easy to over mix this dough - lethal for pie crust.

If over mixed you will have cardboard not pie crust.)

Mix quickly until water is incorporated and dough leaves the sides of the bowl.

Divide into two balls, wrap with plastic wrap and rest in refrigerator or you may freeze it.

Roll out between two layers of floured wax paper, peel off top and bottom wax paper and place in buttered pan.

SIX OF DIAMONDS

(A MOVE)

No Fat Chocolate Cake

- 2-1/2 cups flour
- 2/3 cups cocoa
- 1-1/2 tsp baking power
- 1 tsp baking soda
- Sift together and set aside
- 1-1/4 cup fat free sour cream or 1-1/8 cup fat free buttermilk
- 1/4 cup hot water
- 2 egg whites
- 1 egg yolk
- 1-1/2 cup light brown sugar packed
- 1 tsp vanilla

Beat the eggs and sugar until light as possible, takes about 3 minutes.

Add the vanilla

Beat in the fat free sour cream and hot water alternately beginning and ending with the flour-cocoa mixture.

Bake in a low to moderate oven of 300° for 50 minutes depending on your oven, or until done when toothpick inserted comes out clean.

Cake should be moist and not crumbly.

It can be frozen. Cut into servings and place in individual baggies and use an air tight container and freeze.

Then take out one serving at a time to thaw and eat.

No Fat Chocolate Filling;

- Heat 1/4 c. coffee (may use diet 7-up if you don't like coffee)
- Add 1-8 oz. package fat free cream cheese and beat together until smooth.
- Add 2/3 c. cocoa sifted
- l tsp. vanilla and dash of salt
- 4 packets of artificial sugar or to your taste

Beat until smooth; add more liquid if necessary just to make spreading consistency.

It will firm up when cooled.

Spread on cooled cake.

SIX OF HEARTS
(TRUST)

Old Fashioned Sugar Cookies

- 1/2 cup butter
- 1 cup sugar
- Cream well
- Beat in 1 egg (or 2 egg yo l k s.)
- Add 1 tsp vanilla and mix.
- Sift 1-1/2 cups flour
- 1 tsp baking power
- 1/4 tsp salt
- Add to butter mixture and mix well

Can be rolled out on a floured surface,

I drop these from a teaspoon and then use a fork to press down.

Bake on lightly greased pan at 325° for 8 or 10 minutes or until cookies are LIGHTLY browned around the edges. Do not over bake.

Pie Crust

- 1/3 cup Crisco
- 1 cup flour
- 1/2 tsp salt
- 2 to 3 tbsp ice cold water, put ice cubes in it
  to keep cold.

Incorporate with cutter or knives

Knead just to make a ball and when dough can easily leave the sides of the bowl.

Place ball in refrigerator wrapped in plastic to rest 30 min.

Roll out on floured surface.

I am not a competent pie crust maker and have to put my dough between two pieces of waxed paper. I find it easier to turn the paper and roll into a circle and peel the paper off to get this delicate stuff into the pie pan without destroying it.

SIX OF CLUBS

(CHANGE OF PLANS)

Recipe For Cake Decorating

- 1/2 cup Crisco
- 1/4 cup cold water
- 1 tsp vanilla,
- Place it in the water and add to
- 1 pkg. powdered sugar

Beat until very smooth.

Place any coloring using food dye if desired

Place in the cake decorating bag fashioned with the desired tip and squeeze out the desired pattern.

FIVE OF HEARTS
(SOMETHING VERY SOON OR BY CHANCE)

Delicious Chocolate Cake

- Place to soak 3/4 cup of raisins in 1/4 cup of whiskey or water or 7-up and set aside.
- In a bowl mix 3/4 cup butter or margarine or 1/2 cup oil if you do not use butter
- 3/4 cup brown sugar tightly packed
- 1 cup white sugar

Cream the sugars and butter or oil until smooth, very smooth

Add 1-1/2 oz. melted semi-sweet chocolate and beat

Add 2 eggs and beat 3 minutes more

Add 1 tsp vanilla

Sift together:

- 1-3/4 cup flour plus 2 tbsp
- 1/3 cup cocoa
- 2 tsp baking powder
- 1 tsp baking soda
- 1/2 tsp cinnamon

- 1/4 tsp nutmeg
- Add pinch of salt
- Add the sifted ingredients alternately with cup milk

(If you use Soy milk, then dilute it half and half with water or 7-up as Soy milk makes a cake too dense)

Add 1/2 to 3/4 cup chopped Black Walnuts or 1 cup of chopped English walnuts or pecans

Add the soaked raisins, whiskey and all.

Stir with a spoon and place in a buttered and floured pan or use a releasing agent like Pam.

Bake 315 to 325 for 1 hour or until done when a toothpick comes out clean. Cake will be moist but make sure it is done in the middle even if you have to turn the heat down and bake it another 15 minutes. It is a moist, almost chewy cake. I find that it is best to bake it in two pans. Bake a shorter time and prepare for a double layer cake.

It can be frozen for Christmas holidays.

Ice with Fudge Icing; or if you prefer, sift powdered sugar over the cake just before serving.

FIVE OF DIAMONDS

(CONFINEMENT)

Butterscotch Pie

- 6 tbsp butter
- 2-1/2 cups scaled milk (place milk in pan and heat, do not boil)
- 3 tbsp corn starch
- 1-1/2 cups brown sugar
- 2 eggs separated, place the white in the refrigerator for meringue
- 1/4 tsp vanilla

Melt the butter and brown sugar together and cock until a rich brown, do not burn

Then add the scalded milk and let heat until the sugar is dissolved

Beat the 2 egg yolks slightly, add the cornstarch to the eggs and pour the milk mixture over it gradually, stirring constantly, cooking.

Add 1/4 tsp vanilla, and cook until thickened, pudding consistency. Cool it a little first, stirring do not let skin form. Pour into a baked pie shell, cover with meringue and brown as below.

MERINGUE

Beat chilled egg whites until stiff, dry froth

Beat in 2 tbsp of sugar for each egg, SLOWLY, and continue to beat the egg whites and sugar until meringue is very stiff and will hold peaks, but is still glossy and creamy consistency.

Add 1/2 tsp vanilla

Cover pie with meringue

Bake 300 or less (slow oven) until meringue is a tender brown.

FIVE OF SPADES

(VISIT – OR VISITOR)

Pineapple Upside Down Cake

Place 1/2 cup butter in pan you are to bake in and melt the butter.

Add 1 cup brown sugar and cook until lightly caramelized.

Place well drained pineapple slices in pan.

Set aside

- 3 eggs separated
- 1 cup sugar
- 1/2 cup pineapple fruit juice, unsweetened
- 1/2 tsp vanilla

Sift:

- 1 cup flour
- 1 tsp baking powder
- 1/2 tsp salt

Beat egg whites until stiff – set aside

Beat egg yolks until light

Cream in sugar

Add the juice alternately with flour and baking powder

Add the vanilla

Fold in the stiffly beaten egg whites

Pour batter over fruit and brown sugar in pan

Bake 325 for 30 minutes or until cake is done when tested.

If using toothpick, insert only into cake.

Sea Foam Icing:

- 2 cups brown sugar (light, not dark brown)
- 1 cup water

Combine brown sugar and water until smooth

Then cook without stirring over MEDIUM heat until the syrup strings a substantial hair when dropped from a teaspoon

While syrup is cooking

- Beat 2 egg whites until stiff
- Add 1/8 tsp cream of tartar
- Pinch of salt

Egg should stand in peaks

When syrup strings a hair, then slowly pour the syrup into the stiffly beaten egg whites while continuing to beat with the mixer.

When all the syrup is incorporated, change to a spoon and beat by hand till the icing loses its shine, but does not crack or crystallize.

Quickly pour over the cake and spread.

FIVE OF CLUBS

Sour Cream Coffee Cake

- 2-1/2 cup flour
- 2-1/2 tsp baking powder
- 1/2 tsp baking soda
- 1/2 tsp salt
- 1 cup sour cream (fat free is okay)
- 1-1/2 tsp vanilla
- 1 cup butter (to reduce fat use ½ cup Wesson oil – equally good)
- 1-1/4 scant cup white sugar
- 3 extra large eggs

Filling and topping:

- 1/2 cup chopped walnuts
- 1-1/2 tsp ground cinnamon
- 1/4 cup sugar
- 2 tbsp brown sugar

Sift dry ingredients and set aside

Combine sour cream and vanilla and set aside

Beat the shortening for 3 minutes. Then add the sugar in 2 stages and beat each for

3 minutes

Add the eggs one at a time and when all are in, beat for 3 minutes.

You are trying to put air in the cake. Don't worry. It will come out light and tender even though it has a filling.

On low speed, beat in ½ of the flour mixture

Then incorporate the sour cream and vanilla, and add the other half of the flour

Pour half of the batter into a prepared pan, buttered and floured or sprayed with Pam.

Sprinkle half of the nut and sugar mixture over it.

Pour the remainder of the batter over the filling

Top with the other half of the nuts

Bake in a moderate oven until topping is melted and crispy and toothpick comes out clean when inserted in cake.

FOUR OF HEARTS

(IMMEDIATELY A MESSAGE)

Lemon Meringue Pie

Separate 4 eggs, put 2 egg whites in one bowl, and 2 in another bowl.

They are stiffly beaten and used separately.

Beat 4 egg yolks with ½ cup sugar

Add juice of 2 lemons

Cook in double boiler till just thick, stirring

Beat 2 of the egg whites till stiff with ¼ cup sugar

Add the egg whites to the hot mixture by adding a little of the hot yolks to the white, incorporate gently and then add rest of hot mixture into the whites.

Pour lemon mixture into a baked pie shell.

Beat the other two egg whites till they foam, then

Add 1/4 cup sugar SLOWLY while continuing to beat till stiff.

Spread on pie.

Bake 300 for 15 min. or till lightly **brown**

Banana Nut Loaf (Makes 2 Loafs)

- 1-3/4 cup flour
- 2-1/4 tsp baking powder
- 1/2 tsp nutmeg
- 3/4 tsp cinnamon (generous)
- 1/2 tsp salt
- 3/4 cup shortening (if oil is used, reduce to 1/2 cup plus 2 tbsp)
- 3/4 cup sugar (scant)
- 1 tsp vanilla
- Juice of 1/4 lemon of 1/2 tsp lemon zest optional
- 1-2 eggs beaten with a fork
- 2 ripe bananas cut up
- 1/2 cup nuts (generous English walnuts

Sift dry ingredients and set aside

Cream shortening and sugar till light

Add the vanilla and lemon

Add the eggs one at a time and beat till light

Add pieces of banana and beat in using slow speed of mixer

Spoon in nuts and stir

Pour into 2 loaf pans, this cake rises so fill the pans only half full

Bake low to moderate oven 1 hour. Do not despair. The banana is moist and will prevent loaf from cooking fast. It is done when inserted toothpick comes out clean.

These can be wrapped tightly and frozen. Slice and top with cheese in oven

FOUR OF DIAMONDS

(SUCCESS)

Single Pie Shell

- 1/3 cup Crisco
- 1 cup flour less 1 tbsp
- 1/2 tsp salt
- 2 or 3 tbsp ice cold water, put ice cubes in it
  to keep cold

Incorporate with cutter or knives and cut as long as you want,

Knead just to make a ball after the water has been added.

Place the ball in the refrigerator wrapped in plastic to rest for 30 minutes

Roll out between two sheets of waxed and floured paper.

Bake at 350 – 375 for 10 minutes

Then lower the heat to 300 and cover the edges of the pie crust with pie-edge protectors or strips of aluminum foil.

Bake an additional 40 – 45 minutes or until pie is set

FOUR OF SPADES
(WIRE OR TELEPHONE CALL)

Cream Cheese Wafers

- 1/2 cup butter, softened
- 1 cup grated cheddar cheese – not sharp as the baking makes it too bitter
- 1/2 tsp dry mustard
- 1/8 tsp cayenne pepper or hot sauce
- 1 cup flour plus 2 tbsp

Beat butter till light and fluffy

Beat in cheese and seasonings

Stir in flour

Turn dough out on floured board and knead a few times to incorporate

Roll into a long roll 1-1/2 wide

Wrap in plastic wrap

Refrigerate 1 hour at least

Slice off 1/4" (no thinner)

Bake 300 oven 8-9 minutes

Do not over bake, cheese will burn and wafer is bitter

Wafer should only be golden brown. They are tender, so remove with care and place on wire rack to cool.

THREE OF HEARTS
(INTERESTING RECOVERY)

Cocoa Cake

- Place 1 tbsp of vinegar in a cup of milk and set aside. You may use buttermilk if you have it, or you may use commercial sour cream instead of the sour milk in this recipe.
- 3/4 cup butter
- 1 cup brown sugar
- 1 cup white sugar
- Cream well
- Add 1 egg and
- 2 egg yolks

Set the 2 egg whites aside

Cocoa Icing:

- Sift 9 tbsp of cocoa
- Add cocoa to the mixture
- Sift 1-3/4 cups flour
- 1-1/2 tsp baking power
- 1 tsp baking soda

- Add dry ingredients alternately with sour milk.
- Beat for 1 minute
- Add 1 tsp vanilla

Pour into 2 layer pans, buttered and dusted with flour or sprayed with Pam.

White Icing:

- 2 cups white sugar
- 1 cup water

Cook over medium heat until it strings a hair when dropped from a teaspoon.

Watch the liquid as it drops off.

The syrup is done when the last drop leaves a long steady string behind it.

If it drops in "sheets" or "gobs," you have cooked it too long and your icing will crystallize and crack.

You now have made candy. Forget the icing, eat the candy, and start over.

THREE OF CLUBS
(CHANGE)

Butter, Egg and Milk Cake

- 1/2 cup shortening
- 1 cup sugar
- 2 eggs beaten well
- Sift together
- 1-1/2 cup flour
- 2 tsp baking powder
- 1/2 tsp salt
- 1/2 cup milk plus 2 tbsp
- Add 1/2 tsp vanilla in the milk and stir

Cream shortening and sugar and beat with beater until very smooth

Add the beaten eggs and beat for 3 minutes

Add flour alternately with the vanilla milk

1 or 2 pans can be used, your preference

Bake 2 pans 300 for 25 minutes, or 1 pan 300 for 45 – 50 minutes until tests done

Best Applesauce Cake

Sift together and set aside

- 1-1/3 cup flour
- 2-1/2 tsp baking soda
- 1 tsp cinnamon
- 1/2 tsp nutmeg
- 1/2 tsp salt
- 1/4 tsp ground cloves
- 1/2 cup shortening
- 1-1/3 cup brown sugar tightly packed
- 1 or 2 eggs
- 1 cut tart applesauce (do not recommend chunk applesauce as the chunks will sink to the bottom of the cake
- 1/2 cup raisins (keep raisins in a freezer zip lock bag and freeze the, thus keeping them soft.)
- 1/2 to 3/4 cup English walnuts

Cream shortening and sugar

Add the eggs one at a time and beat until airy

Stir in the applesauce alternately with the flour mixture using about 3 stages

Scrap edges and bottom of the bowl often, things get gooey

Add the nuts and raisins

Pour into a prepared pan round or oblong or 2 loaf pans

Bake at 300 for 40 minutes. Then reduce temperature to 250 and continue baking until done when toothpick comes out clean.

Ice with chocolate icing, white icing or dust with powdered sugar.

THREE OF DIAMONDS

(WEDDING – OR REGARDING MARRIAGE)

Moist Chocolate Cupcakes

Boil the liquid

Add powdered cultured buttermilk. Blend for cooking

Baking available in a can at your grocery store.

Place together in a bowl

- 1/4 cup butter
- 1/4 cup cocoa
- 1 cup sugar
- 2-1/2 tbsp buttermilk powder
- Add 2/3 cup boiling water and beat until smooth
- Add sifted dry ingredients and beat until lumps are gone
- 1-1/2 cup flour (less 2 tbsp. if you live in a dry climate)
- 1/4 tsp salt (optional)
- 1/2 tsp baking powder
- 1 tsp baking soda

Beat with a fork

- 1 egg
- 1 tsp vanilla

Add the egg and vanilla to the batter and beat until creamy

Fill prepared cupcake tins only half full. (These cakes rise)

Bake 20 minutes in moderate oven 325 or when done as tested.

They keep well frozen. Place each cupcake in a baggie and place them in an airtight container.

TWO OF HEARTS
(NEW EXCITEMENT)

Divinity Candy

- 2-1/2 cups sugar
- 1/2 cup boiling water
- 2 egg whites – stiffly beaten

Boil syrup until it strings a substantial hair when dropped from a teaspoon.

Add the syrup to the stiffly beaten egg whites in a slow stream while continuing to beat the egg whites

Then beat by hand until the candy is no longer glossy

Pour into buttered square dish or pan

Cut into desired size candies

Cool

You can also add 1/4 tsp vanilla if you like.

Note: For the incorporation of syrups into egg whites, use your electric mixer instead of hand mixer. Use the wire whip attachment. It is done in a third of the time.

TWO OF DIAMONDS
(SPEEDILY)

Refrigerator Cookies

- 1 cup shortening
- 1-1/2 cup brown sugar (light only)
- 1 cup nuts, chopped or dates or raisins (your choice)
- 2 eggs
- Sift: 3 cups flour
- 1 tsp soda
- ½ tsp salt
- 1 tsp vanilla

Cream shortening and sugar till smooth

Add eggs and beat well

Add sifted dry ingredients

Add nuts or raisins or date, etc

Form into 2 rolls and cover with plastic wrap

Refrigerate until firm

Slice 1/4" in the amount of cookies you need and return the roll to the refrigerator

Bake moderate oven till just golden brown

TWO OF CLUBS
(TRIP)

Non Cooked Stuffed Dates

- 1 – 12 oz. package of dates, pitted.
- Stuff with: 1 cup powdered sugar
- 1/4 cup nuts cut into small pieces
- 1 tbsp whiskey
- 2 tsp soft butter

Mix together so it holds its shape

Cut the dates down the middle in a not-too-long slit.

Fill with a small pinch of the nut mixture that you roll in your palm to make a ball, then pack into the date.

Roll in powdered sugar.

TWO OF SPADES

(REST)

Modern Taste Fruit Cake (Makes About 5 Loaves)

Heat oven to 275 – 280

Have many loaf pans ready as you will use the empty one for liners, stacking pans.

Place on piece of wax paper cut to fit just the bottom of the one pan used for the cake. This

makes it easier to get the cake out.

Fruits:

- 2 cups dates, pitted and cut up
- 2 cups reasonably large pieces of English walnuts
- 2 cups raisins
- 1 small container 8 oz. of commercial candied mixed fruits
- 1 small container of candied cherries and candied pineapple Buy 2, one for in the cake, one for the top decorating

Sprinkle 1/4 cup flour over and stir to coat the pieces.

Set aside.

Sift:

- 4 cups flour
- 3 tsp cinnamon
- 4 tsp baking powder
- 1/2 tsp ginger
- 1/2 nutmeg
- 1/2 tsp allspice
- 1/2 salt

In large bowl with mixer, cream until very smooth

- 1-3/4 cup shortening (if use oil reduce the fat content, use 1-1/2 sticks of butter and 1/4 cup oil. Do not use olive oil or canola oil, it will not rise properly. I use Wesson oil which is soy.)
- 1-1/2 cup white sugar
- 6 eggs, beat in one at a time
- 1-1/4 unsweetened pineapple juice, add alternately with the flour and spice mixture

Next phase:

Pour mixed batter over the fruits and incorporate using wooden spoons.

Fill loaf pans only half full. This cake rises.

Stack the filled pans into 2 or 3 empty pans to reduce burning.

Place cookie sheets under the pans and loose lids over the tops.

Bake 280 for about 17 or 18 minutes. Remove the cakes and decorate with candied pineapple, cherries and large pieces of nuts. If you skip the baking a little first step, your decorations will sink into the cake and be lost.

Return to oven at 275 and bake 1 hour or until done when toothpick comes out clean. Try to miss any fruits.

When almost done remove the lids and let cakes lightly brown on top.

Cool. Remove from pans. Douse with 1/2 oz. whiskey. Wrap securely.

They may be frozen, but must be air tight.

JOKER OF DIAMONDS

Praline Cake

Sift 1 cup cake flour with

- 1-1/2 tsp baking powder
- 1/8 tsp salt
- Cream ½ cup butter
- 2/3 cup sugar
- Add ½ tsp vanilla

Separate 2 eggs. Beat the egg yolks and then add them. With a clean beater, beat the egg whites until stiff and set aside

Add dry ingredients alternately with ¼ cup milk.

Add the egg whites last and fold them in

Pour into well greased pan. Bake 300 about 25 – 30 minutes.

Remove from the oven and coat the cake with the following topping.

Praline Topping:

- 2 tbsp butter melted in skillet
- Add 1 cup brown sugar
- 1 well beaten egg
- 1 tbsp flour

Cook over low heat 3 to 5 minutes stirring

Remove from heat and add 1 tsp vanilla and ¾ cup nuts

Pour over the top of cake while still warm and return to oven baking for another 5 – 7 minutes until coating becomes solid.

JOKER OF SPADES

Easy Oil Pie Crust

- 1-1/2 cup flour
- 1/2 tsp salt
- 1-1/2 tsp sugar
- Mix together in the middle of a pie pan
- 1/2 cup oil, less 2 tbsp. (not olive oil)
- 2 tbsp milk

Mix together with a fork

Pour oil mixture into the flour mixture and stir with a fork.

Then push the mixture around with your fingers to fit the pie pan.

Do not pack, just push and flute the top around the edge.

Bake in 325 oven until just light brown, do not burn.

Cool completely

JOKER OF HEARTS

Champagne Punch – Non Alcoholic

- 1 quart club soda
- 1/2 cup frozen orange juice concentrate
- 1 lemon juiced
- Squirt of lime
- 1 cup grapefruit juice, may use grapefruit soda if desired. Otherwise squeeze a grapefruit
- 1 to 2 cups apple juice or mild apple cider
- Use artificial sweetener to taste

Use 2 packages

Serve in punch cups with ice

JOKER OF CLUBS

Punch From The Cotton Patch

Unsweetened pineapple juice, I use 46 oz. can

Mash well 3 or 4 nice bananas and ·add to the pineapple juice immediately so they will not turn brown.

Add twice as much club soda as pineapple juice or to your taste. If you add too much, you dilute the juice flavor.

Place in bowls, cover / freeze. Good to make the night before.

To serve, dump out one or two of the bowls into your punch bowl and allow to thaw into a slushier consistency.

Leave it alone and as the evening goes on, it wiɪl thaw and become more liquid.

Add more frozen bowls to the liquid.

Pineapple Variation:

Add club soda to frozen pineapple sherbet and stir some as the sherbet will float.

Allow the sherbet to melt.

Everyone stirs it as they serve themselves.

Dear reader,

We hope you enjoyed reading *Cooking By The Cards*. Please take a moment to leave a review, even if it's a short one. Your opinion is important to us.

Discover more books by Rena Winters at https://www.nextchapter.pub/authors/rena-winters

Want to know when one of our books is free or discounted? Join the newsletter at http://eepurl.com/bqqB3H

Best regards,

Rena Winters and the Next Chapter Team

ABOUT THE AUTHOR

Multi-talented Rena Winters has enjoyed an outstanding career in the entertainment industry as a writer, talent, producer, production executive and as a major TV and Motion Picture executive.

Her writing ability won the coveted Angel Award for the "outstanding family TV special, **"How to Change Your Life"**, which she co-hosted with Robert Stack. She wrote the two hour script (and co-produced) for **"My Little Corner of the World"**, winner of the Freedoms Foundation and American Family Heritage awards.

Feature films include **"The Boys Next Door"**, **"KGB, the Secret War"**, **"Charlie Chan & the Curse of the Dragon Queen"** and **"Avenging Angel"**.

Her producing credits include **"The Juliet Prowse Spectacular"** for 20th Century Fox, **"Sinatra – Las Vegas Style"** and **"Peter Marshall – One More Time"**, which produced a best selling soundtrack album.

As Executive Vice President, she headed the entire USA operation for the international entertainment giant, Sepp-Inter, producers of TV Series, TV Specials, Feature Films and all areas of merchandising for their animated entities including **"The Smurfs"**,

"**Flipper**", "**Seabert**", "**The Snorks**" and "**Foofur**" (all Emmy Award winners) plus "**After School Specials**" for CBS-TV.

Author of the bestselling book "**Smurfs: The Inside Story of the Little Blue Characters**" currently available on Amazon and Kindle and in all book stores.

"**Instead of Therapy**", released October, 2015, an inspirational and uplifting easy reading book for busy people. Praised by the President of the American Authors Association as a must read.

Contributing author to an anthology of patriots and heroes, "**I Pledge Allegiance**", sponsored by the Wednesday Warriors Writers group currently on Amazon and Kindle.

Latest book – "**Target One**" A story about how terrorism escalates in America. Winner 2nd Place Best Fiction 2018 by the Public Safety Writers Association.

Rena is a contributing writer to the "**summerlinww.blogspot.com**" as a member of theSummerlin Writers and Poets Group. She is also a contributing writer to WTT magazine WTTmagazine@gmail.com. She is a former writer/reporter for "**thenowreport.vegas**", an online newspaper.

In addition, Rena has recently completed writing a children's book featuring two rescue cats. She also has a forthcoming cook book for people who don't have time to cook.

Rena Winters was voted one of the "50 Great Writers You Should Be Reading – 2017 and 2018" by The Authors Show.com.

At the College of Southern Nevada, Rena is an adjunct instructor teaching Creative Writing courses. She makes her home in Las Vegas, Nevada and works in her spare time as an editor and ghostwriter.

Cooking By The Cards
ISBN: 978-4-82410-746-6
Mass Market

Published by
Next Chapter
1-60-20 Minami-Otsuka
170-0005 Toshima-Ku, Tokyo
+818035793528

26th September 2021